# HENRIETTA GET-A-BLASTER

## Diane Wilmer Redmond
### Illustrated by Valeria Petrone

Henrietta loved to sing.
She sang in her bath

and in her bed,

she would have sung all day and all night
but people kept throwing things at her.
"DOH, RAY, ME, FAH, SOH, LA, TEE, DO-OOOOH!"

"BE QUIET, HENRIETTA!" roared her mum.
"You're giving me a headache."
"But I love singing," cried Henrietta.

"Well I don't!" snapped her mum.
"You've broken every window in the house
with all your shrieking and warbling.
For goodness sake, girl, give it a rest!"

Henrietta stomped off into the garden.
"At least I can sing out here," she thought
and she opened her mouth like a man-hole.

"DOH, RAY, ME, FAH, SOH, LA, TEE, DO-OOOH!"
she squawked at the top of her voice.

"WHAT A RACKET!" bellowed her dad.
"Honestly that voice of yours could
stop a bus! Now pack it in, Henrietta,
or else!"

8

Poor, poor Henrietta.
All she ever wanted to do was sing but it
upset everybody so much she just
had to stop.

She grew sadder and quieter with every passing day.

"We'll have to do something before she fades away," said her mum.
"A holiday might cheer her up," said her dad.
"Oh, yes!" said her mum. "Let's go on holiday!"

So, off they went on a ski-ing holiday.

To begin with Henrietta was very quiet.
She didn't dare open her mouth in case she
caused an avalanche.

Then one day, on the high, snowy peaks, Henrietta felt so happy she couldn't keep her mouth shut one minute longer.

"DOH, RAY, ME, FAH, SOH, LA, TEE, DO-OOOH!"
she bellowed.
The high peaks and deep valleys echoed and
shook with her song.

"DOH-DOH!
RAY-RAY!
ME-ME!
FAH-FAH!
SOH-SOH!
LA-LA!
TEE-TEE!
DO-OOOOOH!"

"YIKES!" thought Henrietta. "This is it!"
She covered her eyes and waited for an avalanche . . .
but nothing happened.

Nothing cracked.
Nothing moved.
Nothing blew away
and NOBODY told her off!

Henrietta couldn't believe her luck.
"WOWEE!" she yelled.
Everyday she went back to exactly the
same spot and sang her heart out.

"Yodel he-hi and yodel he-low,
I can warble all day and let myself go.
With a tra-la-la-LAHHHH!
And a he-hi-ho-HOOOH!
There's nobody here, just me and the snow!"

Henrietta had never
been so happy
in her life.

Soon everybody knew who she was, especially
Fritz, the cable-car driver, who passed her
every morning.

"Ya, ya! Very good!" he called from his car.
"Sing us another, Henrietta. Tra-la-la!"

They yodelled back and forth across the valley
and had a lovely time.

Then one day Fritz's cable car stopped dead.
It swung up and down, up and down, in the icy
cold wind, and all the passengers started to
feel ill.
"Help! Help!" they screamed, but of course
nobody could hear them.

Then Fritz saw Henrietta.
"Please help us, Henrietta!" he shouted.

"Dear me," dithered Henrietta. "What can I do?"
Suddenly she had a brilliant idea.

Her dad had always said her voice could stop a bus, so why not a cable car too? "I'll have a bash!" thought Henrietta and she opened her mouth so wide you could have walked clear around her tonsils.

"DOH, RAY, ME-EEEEE!" she started and the cable car moved forward, just the teeniest bit.
"Ya, ya! Very good," called Fritz.
"More singing. More! More!"

Henrietta sucked in a mouthful of air and
carried on.
"FAH, SOH, LA TEE-EEEE!" she boomed and the
cable car shot along.
"More tra-la-la!" squeaked Fritz. "Louder, LOUDER!"

Henrietta gulped in more air for the
last blast and sang so loudly she thought
the top of her head might pop off.
"DO-OOOOOOOOOOH!" she screeched.

The cable car zoomed to the mountain top
and stopped-BONG!
"HOORAY!" yelled Henrietta.

Everybody hugged her.
Everybody loved her.
"Please stay with us, ya?" begged Fritz.
"And sing your beautiful, beautiful songs."
"No," said Henrietta. "I couldn't do that.
I'd miss my mum and dad."

But every year after that Henrietta went
back to visit Fritz and she sang her songs
on the high mountain tops.
"DOH, RAY, ME, FAH, SOH, LA, TEE, DOH!
she bellowed.
And the sound echoed across the valleys then
rolled away into the big, blue sky where it
was no more than a w-h-i-s-p-e-r . . .!